FAMILY OF MIRRORS

PREVIOUS COLLECTIONS:

Immigrants of Loss
Heirloom
The Ghost of Meaning
Once or Twice
April in Nanjangud

BkMk Press

Dan Jaffe, Director
Rae Furnish, Associate Editor

FAMILY
OF
MIRRORS

G. S. Sharat
Chandra

P O E M S

BkMk Press

1993   *University of Missouri-Kansas City*

Acknowledgments are due to the following magazines and periodicals where some of these poems first appeared:

Antigonish Review (Canada), *Ariel* (Canada), *Chariton Review, Chelsea, Forum, Gila Review, Greenfield Review, Hawaii Literary Arts Review, The Laurel Review, London Magazine* (England), *The Nation, New Letters, North American Review, Outposts Quarterly* (England), *The Partisan Review, Ploughshares, Poet & Critic, Regulator, Slackwater Review, Weber Studies.*

The following have been anthologized: "Chinaman's Hat, North Shore, Oahu," in *Kansas City Outloud II* (Ed. by Dan Jaffe), BkMk Press, UMKC, Kansas City, Missouri; "Hawaiian Zen Fleas," in *North of Wakulla*, Anhinga Press, Tallahassee, Florida; "Confusion," in *Decades* (Ed. by Robert Stewart & Trish Reeves), New Letters, UMKC, Kansas City, Missouri; "Mount Pleasant, USA," in *Out Of This World* (Ed. by Gary Gildner), Iowa State University Press, Iowa; "Still Kicking in America," in *New World of Literature*, W.W. Norton.

Book & Jacket Design: Thomas Zvi Wilson & Michael Annis
Typography: Michael Annis

LIBRARY OF CONGRESS
Library of Congress Cataloging-in-Publication Data

Sharat Chandra, G. S., 1935-
  Family of Mirrors : poetry / by G. S. Sharat Chandra
    p.   cm.
  ISBN 0-933532-90-3 : $12.00 cloth
  1. Family—India—Poetry.   I. Title
PR9499.3.S45F35   1993
  821—dc20   93-325
                                                          CIP

 Financial assistance for this book has been provided by the Missouri Arts Council, a state agency.

for my son Bharat
(and in loving memory of Isaac Bashevis Singer)

RUNAWAY SISTER

"No one can stop me! I'm running away!"
would thunder my sister
up & down the staircase
in the best tradition of Maureen O'Hara,
her tin suitcase jammed with cosmetics, underwear;
she had failed the finals once again.
I kept watch at the window
while her best friends urged her
to catch the bus to Bombay
before the results were posted
in the Nanjangud newspaper.

The last year of her schooling,
after failing three times
she won a certificate in acting,
married our neighbor the insurance salesman
cum part-time ventriloquist.
In her fifties now,
her Garbo eyes are dim behind glasses,
the hair she wore in plaits to her wedding
is trimmed like a hedge,
movie magazines held by rubber bands
are shelved high beside puppets
& policy holders.

A few blocks from the house,
near the bus stop Hollywood restaurant,
a ticket agent in tarnished khaki
promises you discount fares,
& for a slight bribe his word
not to tell anyone where you went
until your first movie is a box-office success.

FACTS OF LIFE

My father, teetotaler, vegetarian,
took two baths a day,
one at dawn the other
before his evening obeisance
to lord Shiva at the temple.

Cleanliness of forms,
the given and the gifted,
adherence to principles,
honesty, truth, purity,
were things he'd die for.

Yet he died of a malignancy
whose virtue was pillage,
whose form spread
from viscera to vision,
from body to soul.

Now he who loved roses
lies buried within limits
of his caste's cemetery
by the river Kabini
where the banyans sway,

where transients and pilgrims
come to celebrate Shiva's victory
over one demon or another.

THE HAMPER

It was old for it was there
before my eldest brother was born,
for he says as a baby
he used to sleep in it,
watch my mother fold her wash
while he played hooky
with its sliding door and wire mesh
or peed into the shirts and blouses
he had slept upon cushioned
as a lord spoiled rotten.

Made out of mahogany, it was sturdy
enough to hold me when we played
caged games from movies.
My sisters, muddy towels around their heads
danced round and round rubbing
their bellies, chanting of the pot
where I'd be steamed soft as a snail.
I remember shaking the hamper's frame
asking for reprieve, offering bribes.
When all words failed,
I'd yell for Tarzan loud as the Jesuits,
until herding elephants the great one came
in the guise of my brother,
to chase the gaudy headed tribe,
while our elephant, the bamboo chair,
roped for a quick climb stood nearby.
The dazed eyes hidden under the bed
prayed we leave Africa
without ripping their face.

When we moved from town to town,
the hamper always accompanied us,
still sturdy, though the wire mesh
tugged and punched showed bulges,
the wires hung out and the lid came loose.
As we grew, new machinery replaced the old,
the hamper moved to the back porch then the yard
where it became a post office, then a rock depository.
When my youngest sister nagged her way,
her pups took over and tore it
until the frame broke.
In a short while,
the hamper lost all shape
hunched under a tree next to a wood pile
for birds and squirrels,
then they too lost interest.

It was thrown I forget when and where,
but I remember
when I was four or five,
hiding inside it
under a tent of flowered bed sheets,
faking a forlorn cry.
When my mother found me
she held me prancing wild,
nose in my belly her quick kisses
wandering over my shirtless body.

MOUNT PLEASANT, USA

at night
I'm a man surprising himself
in sleep a slight stirring of the curtains
at the window the flies kiss
the bottles to their heart's content
the glass
is stiff with their chanting

each night I shift
to another place
to another failure
in Iowa I dream of Nanjangud
my mother
the illiterate waiting
her eyes gone dim her hair
off to nowhere . . .

given up on sons given up on herself
waiting the night for the day
to be over for the day to begin

in the bars
of Chicago in the scowl
of Mount Pleasanteans in the handshake
of friends in the flashback
of promises in my exile

the cage I carry is the cage I made

MY DAUGHTER'S NEW DOG

— for Anji

I don't like to be licked
by a pup in the morning
while I'm still in bed,
especially by a black mutt
who gorges on my french bread,
doesn't bark at strangers,
sleeps all night instead.

Prompted by my daughter
whom he licks each dawn
to a radiant new way,
he's here beside me
half eager, half afraid.

Go ahead, she says
without asking for my consent,
he jumps on the bed,
nuzzles me quickly by the neck,
then he's down beside her
wagging an acceptance.

My daughter thanks me with a kiss,
then they're off to other tussles,
I drive to my office
rubbing my neck of the beast's bristles,
while the petals of her kiss
spread from a child's ways
to the child in me, now awake.

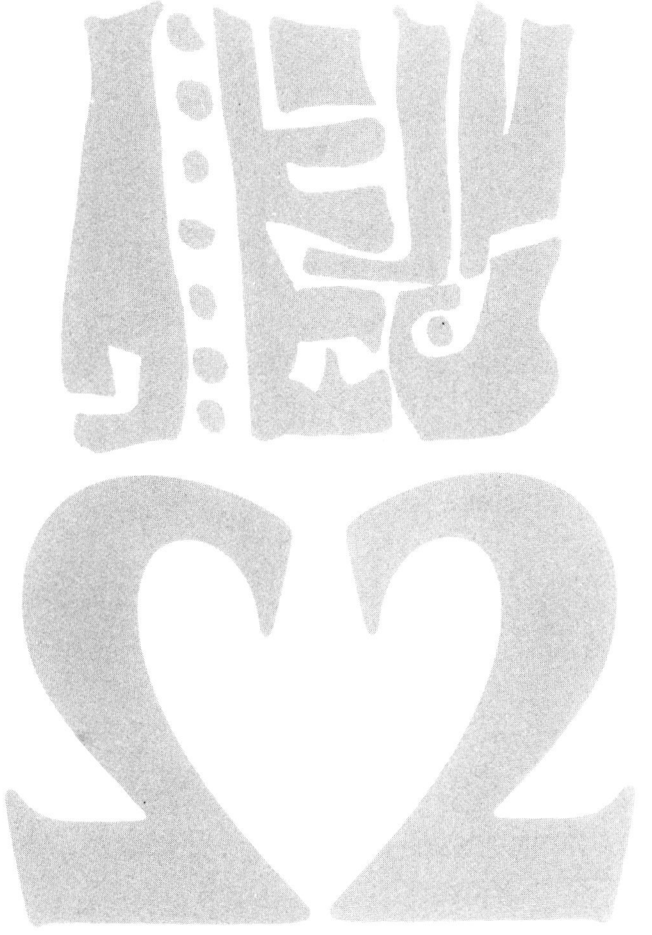
22

THIS POEM

This poem is the chronicle of the ruthless
who grabbed it by its hungry gullet
erased its memory

This poem is how one evil leads to another
how one impure breath teaches
others to consume themselves

This poem is men in beer halls   motel rooms
jet planes   bowling alleys
trying to master it

This poem is the mouth the bomb was shoved in

This poem is children who died
without an oral tradition
when their heads went off

This poem glows forever on a hard planet

This poem is my mouth in splinters
chew it well brother

FABLE OF THE TALKER

He was born while the oracles
withered in their tongues.
He talked his mother to his father's penis;
wishful, unfailing were words
he propelled as sperms—
he was behind them
prompting his own preferred game
with a mouth that diminished everything.

Quickly, they dispatched him to school.
He went into books then out,
he ran with words
faster than the words could,
then he ran some more.

Growth was a word he outgrew easily,
love, song, affair,
he married them, albeit singly:
when they took him to courts,
he talked them into a corner,
the corner to keep them there.

Success was a word
wagging between his legs,
fame a bone he needn't contend.
When assassins ambushed him,
he talked their weapons out of aim;
he swallowed the men
in their foils shamed.

The world surrendered.
Its only hope, Time.
When he heard that, he laughed,
wrapped himself in silence and set a trap.

THE FALL OF EIFFEL TOWER

(Ad for Bell Telephone shows the Eiffel Tower
on the back of an empty town)

This is an ad which illustrates
how to bring over there over here,
here being this small town
you'd otherwise will not give a damn,
for it's always under a by-pass
or the wrong detour you make for gas
as you follow highways everywhere.

On the main street nothing moves,
the sidewalks are empty,
the litter bin latched to the lamp post
and the mail box beg for sparrows,
parking meters gape tongue-tied
by the boulevard of potted elms.

This, the U.S.A.,
to which no one returns
that Ma Bell chose,
like Icarus pods balanced in homage
for the Eiffel Tower to fall from sky.

Hello, am I reaching someone there.

FABLE OF A THREE YEAR OLD

— for Shali

A hole is something you make to grow.
Something in the ground a hole
is made for flowers to grow.
A hole is also made for dead bodies
to lay quietly when they're dead
so they don't get up & scare everybody.
Sometimes I get thirsty in the night
but I hate to get up cuz I'm scared
of dead bodies who come
into the kitchen to drink milk.
One night I saw a dead body eating
the chocolate cake my Mom had made for my birthday.
She ate the best part like the bear's nose,
its M&M eyes, its ears which were vanilla.
I saw this in my room where I was sleeping
with my eyes wide open and the dead body
was sitting in the kitchen in my chair
eating the cake and making a lot of mess.
I think this dead body lives in our backyard,
that's where she went after eating my cake.
I told this to my toothfairy so she fixed up
my cake so Mom didn't have to make another one.
Also my toothfairy got very mad at the dead body,

put a huge rock over the hole
and told her not to do it ever again.

My brother says dead bodies can make
other holes to come out if they wanted to,
the only way to keep them down is to hide
behind a door and hit them.
My dead body isn't such a bad girl,
she was only hungry and likes birthday cakes.
I told my toothfairy to give her lots
of chocolate cake when her birthday comes
so she doesn't have to eat in our kitchen.

My brother says he has seen dead bodies
moving all over the house in the night,
looking at my door and he knows the magic word
which will make them disappear,
but he won't tell it to me
cuz I don't tell him
where I hid his baseball bat.

FABLE OF THE COARSE ROSE

The path of the rose was uncharted.
It began to seek itself out.
It grew a sententious hand.
The hand flattened each leaf each thorn each petal
Until the rose was flat as a highway.
Bees and butterflies got lost on it.
The hand patrolled the rose day and night,
It beat the hell out of vagrants and hitchhikers,
Cats and dogs ran from it
Yowling and limping.

No amount of warning could keep everyone away,
Since it was hard to tell
Which was the rose with the spanking hand,
Since all roses imitated one another
Though they were not equipped with the hand:
One had to risk his ass to find out.
It became ludicrous to speak to strangers
Of one's experience with rose slaps,
Or to convince the world to alter
Its conception of roses,
Until men of learning fresh from a beating
Revised their thoughts and feelings,
Until Shakespeare was removed from his grave
And buried next to Frankenstein.

FABLE OF HEARTS

Our daddy isn't tall,
our mom is taller,
but she makes herself small
when he's standing.
We draw hearts for our dad.
You can make hearts
with plastic, cardboard,
glue, even jelly,
but crayoned hearts
are the real thing.
They teach you
what your parents don't.
When we sell our hearts
to our dad,
he gives them to our mom,
she sticks them
on the refrigerator
where they don't stay.
We don't like them
on our refrigerator.
The best thing would be
if we were to draw
the secretest heart
with many colors
and one door.
We can hide in it
until they find us.

CHILDREN

Let me say this love,
we've passed into units
by their own bodies glowing,

do not weep
they now seek others
with no thought for you or me.

Rejoice in what life meant
in its wheat of joy,
the millet of sorrow,

for you see our weighted sighs,
in their young bodies
holding wise.

HAWAIIAN ZEN FLEAS

Miniscule bandits against spiritual sagacity,
they don't bite you,
at least not rightaway,
in your thighways they sit and meditate:
you begin to tingle,
you master the lotus position
sensing the coming itch in silence.
There are three of them
in the scope of your bi-focals:
speak no flea, see no flea, hear no flea,
all held still in the bulge of your flesh
doing nothing.

Just for the sake of them
as if the wisdom of their bite
is already yours,
you wish welts all over your body.
This is what they've been waiting for,
your awakening, your surrender,
if you wish an itch, it wishes the scratch,
why bother.

To regain your sanity
you wink at the three,
think of Jane Fonda:
what would she do if they invaded
the sanctity of her video arch,
surrender? Of course not,
she'd call inspector of Hanes
to fumigate all aerobic crotch.
The thought makes you smile,
the fleas smile back.

You're suddenly fond of them,
you throw away your glasses,
after all, what's a bite
if honorable Zen is doing it.
A little bird inside you begins to sing—
wisdom is coming,
you see the fleas clear as Bodhisatva,
if they want your balls,
give them your balls,
be above it all.

CHINAMAN'S HAT, NORTH SHORE, OAHU

It's Mr. Chang alright,
bent so deep
only his hat is visible.
He was planting rice in China
& got carried away,
before he knew it
he was seeding Kaneoha bay,
nose in waves, hat afloat
while revolutions come and go,
minding his own tranquil thoughts.
Tourists brag how his hat turns
while they zig-zag by his anchored shore.

He doesn't care,
fistful of rice stalk still to be laid,
he dreams what the submerged dream:
giving all land away.

If in the century of his marching
by some unintended error
he angered an emperor
and the descendants of the army
who pursued him are still lurking by
to see him rise giddily godly
in seaweed and coral hair,
be it known that the hat is hollow,
he's not under it suspended with fishes,
he's on the shore grown bald and anonymous
with grandchildren he can scarcely recognize
deep in the folds of his hatless mortality.

HONEY, IT'S SUGARLESS

After a report on
American tourists in China

She greets them with gum
& tourist Chinese—
never mind her accent
they smile,
to be polite is to be noble,
some ancient sage had said—
"Look, they understand!"
She yells to her husband
who has pinned a peasant
against the Great Wall
& hopes for a Panda
to complete the capture.
There's everything in their hotel
to which they're accustomed,
even the waiter looks like
janitor Chua who lives
across from their suburb's
industrial surfeit.

While they're here,
the Tourist Agency has assured them,
the President will not start a war,
bandits and revolutionaries
would be kept out of their rooms,
Tsing Tao is approved by Budweiser,

in case they catch anything,
they'd be treated in Switzerland.

This is their last night,
they're happy the Chinese band
plays Marimba and Pennsylvania Polka,
they dance, they cuddle,
their cigarettes swirl shapely as fiddles,
from their air-conditioned window
the Great Wall curves like a dragon
bathing its scales in the moonlight,
they cannot see the guards
hobbling with American gum
stuck to their soles.

AT AN IOWA CITY BAR

The way
he sits talking about Zen
in his cold & detached style
downing scotchafter scotchafter scotch
without taking a leak,
almost makes me believe
in the mystic orient.

CONFUSION

This is confusion translated
from one part of the head to another.
Which part to which is not known,
nor the fact that a head exists
as a strong possibility.

The head immediately says,
I'm not here, I've gone shopping with Marianne Moore
who keeps saying I want to be alone
because I am writing a poem about confusion.
Where is it? I must have misplaced it.

Confusion is defined as because you're here
I can't do a damn thing,
so go away, who are you anyway.
I didn't meet you on the new year,
I met the new year alone.
I remember it clearly because
I spent the night with a red blossom.

Rafael Alberti says,
only married women ask interesting questions
and know when the end of the world is near.
Rafael Alberti did not say this,
I made it up out of sudden clarity
which is occasionally possible
if you don't take more than five minutes thinking it up.
After such a feat, confusion says
you shouldn't answer any questions.

IDENTITIES

They bang seals
of embossed words on my passport—
entries, exits.
On the photograph,
a circle of words
slicing my ear
declares who owns me.

On the last page,
there are countries
I cannot enter,
doors that I may open
only with special permission.

I'm claimed by seals
badgered on pages,
injury upon injury,
fresh blues for arrivals,
healed blues for departures,
the slam bang of bureaucracies.

Someday I'll take my duplicate selves,
give up my face,
wear the untouched name,
disappear between doors.
Then they'll mutter in languages
memorized in orphanages
as to whose baggages they carry,
waking from body to body.

ARS POETICA

After four years
of teaching our checks
to the landlord
the grocer   the doctor
the dentist   the plumber
from bouncing,
my wife bought a jordache
& a leather bag.

I traded the rest
of our family wealth
for a Hathaway patch
& a fifth of Glenfiddich.

Now when we drive
dressed up & drunk
the whole town
nods its head
in praise of poetry.

LOVE RITES

I cut my finger
slicing cucumbers,
I sucked the blood,
she came and kissed
the slices of my hurt,
O my, it felt good.

I cut my finger,
sucked the blood,
I liked the taste.
I wonder now
if I cut another,
would she make haste
to suck it better.

I cut my finger.
It was a bleeding shame
to tell her,
she was gobbling
everything on the plate.
If this be love,
she be vampire,
I be safe bait.

I cut my finger,
looked for a band-aid
which wasn't there
like love when you need it,
so bounteous elsewhere.

I cut my finger
slicing cucumbers,
I got mad and swished it
in the blender,
she asked coyly,
was I cooking a wish
or dishing a murder.

I didn't cut any fingers,
put band-aids over them
just to impress her,
now everyone is doing it.

This is about fingers,
precious love
that ribbons over words
in my written line.
She's wooed by others,
would you be my valentine.

LOVERS

Meeting once again by rendezvous
in this motel,
we sit after making love
indifferent like the burned out lamp.
Nothing has changed in our love or passion
but reason, as always, ducks its head.
Do we go on,
do we have to go on
making and remaking the past to fit a present
which we dream as possible,
we should know better.

You look wonderful,
your travels to the East
have made you exact, intriguing,
you can speak for hours interestingly,
you've stories that can sell.

A rooster crows somewhere,
an early traveller guns his engine,
in the room next to our skin
a toilet is flushed,
the walls tremble,
you draw me closer under the blanket
to check the time on my wrist.
It's still an hour before check-out,
you'll catch that bus,
I'll drive home,
you'll be a passenger on a jet,
I'll be a car on the highway.
Our bodies are made this way,
we bring them together,
graft skin over skin,
but there's always a check-out time,

always bones that never meet
the heir to our darkness.

LOVE POEM

This piece of paper
I was saving is drunk.
It collapses in my hand
like an erection
that reflects too long
on images of sad lovers
that'll never meet again.

Where rages the wind
there I must follow,
says the paper
without any words
to hold it.
It's foolish to lecture
on decorum,
the necessity for poetry,
the art of rescuing
the paramount in the fleeting.

The paper is drunk.
There are no lines,
no stanzas, no images,
no nothing.
Sad lovers part by the sea
having said
their ordinary goodbyes.

LUSTING FOR LONI BALZER

Holding
the questions
in this quiz I made up
to the lust I imagine
in the slit of your eye,
you sit legs spared
so far as to make
a heart thump under a chair,
your dark, insouciant hair
touching the floor,

&
I'm dreaming you
head propped on my pillows,
right breast tipping
the air,
my hand riding the crest
of your curve,
say, to wait like a bird.

Pray, who cares
for incandescent words
in literary tests,
on an ordinary day
with plotless lust
unrehearsed in the air,
as I shift to suffer you poised,
write what you want
to move your thighs at will
with all the answers.

LOVE SONG OF RASHEED THE MAD CAP

Praise to thee great Allah,
For carving my beloved
Pure as the sand of Mecca,
Rarer than the rose rarest.

But Allah,
Why you make her princess
Beyond reach of servant Rasheed?

The suitors are at the palace gate
Hankering after my love-bird.
Her father the Khaleef
Hath proclaimed—
Let eet bee
Who touches the rose tree
The one she marree.

How great you are Allah,
The fat prince of Persia
Fed on lard is passing
Touching not the rose tree.
Hurray Bismillah,
The Nawab of Nokredeet
Has his eye on the balcony
His hands on the box he carree,
He touches not the rose tree.

Marches Ahmed, prince of 7 palaces
Missing the rose tree
By an isle & 14 torches,
O merciful father of horses.

& Zanab Tak-i-Wauk

Takes his walk
Right past the rose tree
O lover of the love famished

With each suitor passing
Touching not the rose tree,
My beloved blushes
Hoping it will be mee,

Guide me then
With hands of strategee,
To the rose tree the rose tree.

UNTIL SOLD DO US PART

Joanna & George, married, mangled,
have bought the house next door,
have moved to the neighborhood
like others before.
Though their marriage is finished
they're sprucing up the building.

George is painting the house
with latex that'll outlast this century,
Joanna cleared the backyard of weeds
for azaleas, myrtle, camellias, peach
to blossom in time next spring
for brokers to get cozy.

Who says a house is not a home?
In these times
of hearts falling short of certainties,
marriages may come apart
but a house keeps its equity.

RAQUEL WELCH READ TOM WOLFE

Raquel Welch read Tom Wolfe
I read Judith Krantz,
it was a platonic relationship
this side of Gucciland.

Raquel was on a non-stop flight
when the controllers walked out,
she ran short of a runway,
I was fishing for trout.

Things went on splendidly,
we were so far from the South
she resembled Gloria Steinem
with a lemon straw in her mouth.

She wore a jumpsuit for dinner
I wore my dhoti grand,
all we talked of was metaphysics,
the space where voyeurs land.

She didn't ask me to swim
I didn't ask her to dance,
we had so much ground to cover
between the sea and sand.

Raquel Welch read Tom Wolfe
I read Judith Krantz,
it was a platonic relationship
this side of Gucciland.

PREPARATIONS

In late August they cross the street
nothing is exchanged between them of the emptiness.
The newspapers pile up everywhere
the moving of the windswept polar caps.
He thought it was a wolf that had peed in the park.
She was busy snipping around the zipper
tracks unlike any events but leading
to openings that reversed on themselves.
She felt the same way about cancer.
The business envelopes once you got used
to their licking felt acknowledged.
So complete is the intensity behind impersonal words,
the clever manipulation of mind over hems.
He thought comings & goings remain
constant like a gardener's hand or General's.
Would it be appropriate to greet one
without reveries on both sides of the Atlantic?
"Ah, now you're picturesque!" she said
pulling the sweater. The bullfinch being
observed looked once in passing,
ah gust! this like any other
a shudder holding its own course.

MOTHS

I.

She said
while she looped her hair

helplessly high
over her tight breasts,

I sat spinning
snares in the bed,

so she hid to undress
in the closet

with the moths:
she came to know

the moth in me
bred also under shelves.

She moved out quickly,
I let her go,

tore her dress
to the outer world

then spun my body
with all my spit

to rise in my chest
the chant of moths,

my father waking
somewhere in a dream,

my brother turning
in the belly of the bulb.

II

We sit in the closet
pretending

we're the one side
of darkness the walls

do not feel.
My brother tries

the red shirt of my father,
the one he hung

on the light bulbs
of strange harbors

to make his women glow
like lanterns of their true country.

Outside my wife drops
her robe humming

into the mirror
her naked dailyness.

She's our secret treasure,
our lookout for moths.

My brother aims
the golf club at her crotch,

the dark in the door ajar
is our wedge of bait,

our fingers drumming
on the flat breast

of the closet switch,
its back & forth nipple.

III.

I've been waiting in the closet
with the moths,

they stir when the lone bulb
flickers then gives up.

I remember my father
grown thin as a cat with cancer,

his quick leap into the birdless air,
the last surge of blood on his spit.

My wandering brother has found his passion
back this spring,

he explains to my wife
the trees that came in the way,

the thin wall of leaves
he mistook for moths.

She laughs softly as she makes tea,
if I touched her back she'd stiffen

to the moths in my sleeves drowsing,
at the cloud of wings if I wave.

IV.

Her daily gestures
naked at the window,

openings of her desire
she wants to cover,

are offerings to the world
in her small darts of eye.

Hair let loose,
head into the dishes

her buttocks seesaw
over the kitchen sink,

within her transparence
we know the silk

tracing the slopes of her vulva.
When she's finished,

she'll draw the blinds,
turn the lights off,

check the doorknobs
and come into the bedroom

to rub fragrance on her skin,
to climb into the mirror

next to the closet
where we practice the range

in our eyes for the dark,
the one perfect leap

we need to dare
in our blind flutter.

V.

Her moans we smother
with a necklace of lips,

father's thigh thrust
over her throbbing,

his right fingers
counting the heaves

of her left nipple,
in the powder smudge

on the mirror,
my brother's sniff:

then she's up & singing
of the blaze in the closet,

guides us there
for one last tango,

unplugs the darkness
to lock our thighs.

She'll catch that plane
to her mother's nest,

where the only dream
is the dream of dead moths.

She'll sleep the winter
hands tucked

under the gargantuan leaf
patched on her quilt.

FICTIONS

Mixing words
on this side of the room.

On the other
her supine body, unclothed,
over the red sofa,
a small wine table,
of course with wine bottle
and a rose.

Wind whistles
through the storm window
where the caulking has withered,
ruffling the drapes,
over her bare calves,
her slightly parted thighs,
her pubic hair.

He's decoding the stillness
as I said,
on this side of the room,
a grenade is hurled,
the light of the half splintered
afternoon shoots
in the sudden gush of air
outwards through the window.

The man across the street
who deals in fictions
stands gaping at his door,
a jogger two stories below
is frozen under shards of glass
that have overtaken him.

Then the distant wail
of a siren
blocks or countries away,
a blind above it is lifted
then dismissed,
the wife of the unnamed
is cooking dinner,
(who was the supine woman?)
The bird is in the oven,
she switches on the television
for the evening news
wrapped heavily in blankets.

STILLNESS

the hours
sullen goats grazing on emptiness
drift mutely to the other side of day

the sun has cast his mid-day net
but doesn't move
to pull in the catch —

a chameleon
two stink bugs stiff after love
a towhee dozing over my patch of impatiens

stillness is making its point
knowing this
the wind plays dead

DREAMERS

It's an easy drift into their domain,
there's no need to bring gifts
or news from the country.
Men sit on benches arranging
nails on windowsills for birds to peck.
There's the smell of hyacinth
in the sawdust on the floor
they've sawed off to let you in.
Their women enter naked
in their Madonna breasts,
they curve their arms around your neck,
their sweet whisperings stay
on your earlobes.

But it's always a half spoken word,
misspelled name, streets that you
do not remember.
Are they tricking you?
Is there really a house that drifts
in halls of wind where they wait,
their lips trembling for your touch.

They say they've been waiting
this way wandering from window to window
as you move from your body.
You could easily fly back to your body,
to the exact space you occupied
under the cool sheets
next to the nightlamp even now shining
through this starlight.

TRIBAL GODDESS

The circassian eye lashes
of this goddess
all by herself across
the bar are unaware
I'm glancing at her.

They flutter
like the wet wings
of a butterfly
afraid of getting stuck
at the margins,
find something to focus
as if her proboscis
uncurled to explore
the labyrinth of ice
at the rim of her drink.

She sucks on the straw,
thoughts ascend
quickly through the narrow
transparency to bubble
with her impossible quest.

She turns radiant,
but the smile on her face
plays the ambiguities
we both know exist:

beauty stated this way
is a premise reckoning
with hidden opposites.

I try ambiguities of my own
into her face.
As if I had entered
her hive of thoughts,
as if my thoughts
grew loud as a spoken field
in the tribe of waitresses,
she disappears
in a flurry of blanks
an unbegun lover,
leaving me to smudges
of noise without a name.

VACANCIES

— for Dan

Out of my body
I take my loneliness,
hang it on the windowsill,
its orphaned tail
limp between opaque glass slits.

I sing of unfettered shoulders
where its tail swung
from bone to barren bone,
from posture to slumped posture,
to play only its sodden self
on the ladder of vacancies:

under my nibbled eyes
the bags I carried
were its bags of witchery.

Distilled of its submerged joy,
my loneliness stares
from its windless orphanage,
take me back, take me back,
I'll shun my blunders,
dangle not my gender.

All too late,
I've opened my shirt
to the flap of its absence,
I've anchored bone
to a family of mirrors.

TAKING STOCK

Counting time has come simply
because this sense of worthlessness
that I've always preserved needs
once more a reassurance.
I've written words, pushed them far,
pulled them from an orbiting leap,
coaxed them to peck in order,
pressed breath to their tunnel of stanzas.

I've rammed images headlong,
thrilled to the whack
of skull bones in blank corridors,
hung words stealthily
behind on trees
gladly for gadflies to retrieve,
walked away from circled ceremonies
where beast pandered to beast.

So far's never been the right preface for so good:
To have written a dozen bright ones
was worth the bewildered wait
for the surfacing, the uncanny clarity,
the simple way judgments were made,
partly or wholly a truth discovered,
through the spinning years.

SCREWS & HINGES

Unable in their freedom
these screws that hold doors
go round and round
as if they weren't held
by hinges

They go round and round
laughing
twirling out of
   grooves
doing pirouettes
hassling each other
slapping heads
embracing
kissing

What will they do
when the dark returns
and orders the doors closed

Grief locked into their eyes
they twist their faces
into to the pool of doors

hinged to the obedience
of opening and closing

VOYAGES

Someone while we sleep
in the soft hues of our longing,
hands cupped against gravity,
boards a sabotaged airplane.

The airplane blows up
briefly high among the clouds,
the dismembered hurtle down
into the dark laps of the sea.

We're dreaming of other things:
reversals in an inconsequential day,
arriving late for something momentous.
We stir, utter a sudden cry.

The aflame plummeting
by the stern of an immutable freighter,
the captain dreaming of his wife.
He had only to lift his head,

but he was trapped to his thoughts,
the slow remembrance
of his wife's familiar body,
the way he'd entice it

after such a long absence,
how the black negligee
with its glittering stars
upon her breasts, he'd undress.

Let's assume
the startled bodies bobbing
face into water beside him
are also dreaming,

for when we wake up
in our beds simply released,
our faces always safe
after the amazing event,

we also live or die
in them without moving,
having felt nothing
outside of our thoughts.

THE GRAIL

Under my feet
in the subterranean,
a procession of ancient pilgrims
is forever chanting for the grail.

I'm running from a hysteria
of gestures,
the relentless bark of words.

Someone skilled in speculations
pulls out a poem from his billfold,
ghosts move quickly by the window
for a fresh whisper.

Around the white sheet
on the dinner table laid with fruits,
the frontier where half bitten
strawberries dipped in sour cream
are already crushed
by a train of mumbo-jumbo,
the gathered alert
to each other like mummies.

The billfold poet finishes,
his women applaud in swirls
as his words fall on the carpet
gently as dollar bills.

Beneath us the pilgrims
mutter like thieves
in a crowded market
after a sack of promises.

THE MUSE

Entering this dream
like a limb of light,
her touch colors my skin,

I'm clothed in this amber
when I turn to kiss her,

something soft and tremulous
as a flower
jumps into my hands.

She goes swishing
as the wind's silver
in a field of mustard flowers.

I see her climb a window
deep within my eye-hold
as if in another country,

the gray pellets of rain
like the half dark ripples
of her robe
moving in the clear,
then in untold shadows.

She climbs to float
in an octagonal kite,
its red string
in the hands of intruders.

NIGHTMARE

Not so much the stare
or the hand
turning the knob,
but your knowing
it's there on a ledge,
behind the door
next to your bed,
quite opaque, quite ready.

Within its folds
you wake
to tell yourself
it passes like a shiver
if you turn to a side,
even blink,
far away children call,
far away a mother answers.

You look at the window,
at the hollow
where tonight it sits
in the breath of the clock,
you know its reach
inching past twelve,
starved for your fifty
in rooms grown so empty.

Sheets thrown, limbs akimbo,
you sink soundless
at the rim of your scream,
asleep beside you

your lover
has thinned to a strand,
you grope to hide
in the shadow of her hand.

TWO WOMEN

The answer to all loneliness
may yet swallow us
as these two women walking
towards each other, heads bent,
these stores boarded up
by the already abandoned gas station,
the road needing bandages,
all this fusing,
and in that line of fusion
as if to answer all misery,
the two women merge into one,
the face you've seen both ways,
half human, half bankruptcy,
breathing hard, its breath looking for answers
at an upward point
of the vanishing ascent.

ANNIVERSARY OF A DROWNING

My father has dived
to the floor of the pond,
turns his eyes to rim
the borders
of the clear green
under the belly
of this world.

He looks at my feet
scuffle, scratch,
grope in sheer obedience
to things he cannot know.

When I pause,
he senses my presence
nosing the ripples
blind as a just born mouse,
my toes gripping
the thin membrane of faith,
his held breath
between words,
and my need to let go.

THE ABSENT

Bells do not ring
when our names are called,

we are the no people
who were once the yes people,
we are China in the back closet,
wash left in the rain
with the wind moving our sex.

Our words are awkward
between forks and knives,
between shadows
on the dinner plates,
we're stones fluttering
in your intimate eyes.

Yet you've given us
a place at your table,
it's a tight place
between crowded chairs,
naked we do not know
if you have us here
to keep yourselves separate.

IN THEIR TORN SHIRTS

Our fathers in their torn shirts
are looking for the last beer can

        because they know
our mothers married us
when we were children

        because our fathers have become
        common like the guy next door

        The last beer can is planning
        a boat trip in the label

        on its ocean for our fathers

        who are disgusted with our mothers
        who gave us the opening in the bed
        swallowed the house key

        Our fathers in their torn shirts
            have thumbs on the ripped throat

        of the last beer can
        they circle the porch to catch us in the red

POETS IN GROUPS

In their photographs,
they stand frozen to permanence.
Only the eyes,
in that fraction of second
when they squint
reveal their fears,
hushed, slanted,
paddled deep into a swirl.

You sense
the birds in their thoughts
sullen on branches sagging with snow,
the monkish light pacing beyond black boughs,
the familiar echoes
in the dream valley,
a boat fishtailing into mist.

How much is hidden and why
is only assumed
like the line
in the subconscious,
their faces, made blank, do not show the depths

in which they're held.

VAN GOGH'S EAR

Think of his ear shooting swiftly
through the century,
soft as an oyster in its bed of crimson
chambers where he lost his sleep,
tremulous, at last come alive
to claim the prize.

Through a soft train of mist
it arrives at Sotheby's,
memory of yellows flaming upward,
the cacaphony of crows
that once strained his manners,
spilled its limits.

If memory speaks,
the odd ear would listen—

'Of the two flowers a man could grow,
I was the one dearest to Van Gogh.'

The aficionados of entries and exits
are banging nails into crates of imitations,
they do not speak about it
until now breathing the dark of an alley,
circling like a moth,
the edge of its healing mellows
driving phantoms frantic.

They are selling his muted excuses.
If he were all ears,
his face stayed unbent,
and the wail in his soul didn't ask
for him to dismember it,
would he have remained valid and whole again?
His face back in grace,

would he have lived beyond that afternoon,
cypresses shooting flames into his fingers?
Crows maligning his temper, eating the uncertain light,
would he have tunneled back
into a foldless sleep,
the terrified whisper
not to dream of the wind's half-hearted ways
around a crystal shutter,
but to awake in a century where riches would claim him,
make his heart in gladness flutter?

Someone knocks on the ear's frameless door,
for it's entering America,
they wish to see the ear's duplicate selves,
riding intact,
to be stamped into a passport.

Auctioneers wait for another chance.

'Of the two flowers a man could grow,
I was the one dearest to Van Gogh.'

The ear tunnels back,
way back into a whore's snicker,
an old hunger claims its anger,
the seams of its scream
pulled apart like a zipper.

SHOPPING WITH AKHMATOVA

Life's work you say,
the essence of myself?
I can't find it,
I've misplaced it,
maybe in America
they've translated it.

I'm Akhmatova,
Anna akhmatova,
this isn't going right,
call me Ann,
hold my arm
don't be foolish.

What's the matter?
If I were dead,
I'd be confused.

Ask interesting questions
about love and waiting,
cuckoos singing in graveyards,
why am I always late.

Stick around
there's enough confusion,
when did you last love me,
eat the peaches,
we're only shopping.

MOON FAREWELL

Being round
was never my idea
of beauty,
why, if you were silver
I minted into a dime
I couldn't buy
a candy bar with
your presidentials missing.

Yet sometimes
I've admired your dieting,
but to chew yourself
half the month
out the slim
of your fingernail
isn't my idea
of elusive & sexy.

I do not know
how many times
you've been caressed
probed & waylaid,
but I know poets
who still swear
you're untarnished,
who'd drown in your glow.

But moon,
let's face it;
you'll soon be replaced
with plastic lunacy
ordering us
to fall in love
under satellite discs
to cybernetic ecstacy.

ISLANDS

This gas station attendant
must be in her twenties,
lighting up at my entrance,
red hair and freckles;
lips curl when she says,
have a nice day;
fingers handing the change
warm the pennies
all the way to the triangle
of softness in my pocket,
her young breasts proud
of the awe in my stare.

Imagine I ask her she says yes,
we drive for miles climbing
the Byzantiums of real estate,
to a place I've dreamed
sunflowers next to a waterpump,
and among clumps of tall weed
she dances like a cardinal
arching out of raindrops;
I hold her spoiled forever,
damn all the lonely who don't.

Yesterday I drove the car empty,
pulled in for a fill up,
must've sensed the codger in me,
called me sir,
boy friend grinning
from his isle of quick lubes,

eyes blank as the weather
slid nickels & dimes on a tray
far as commerce.

And the glass door closed
to the mechanics of springs
and air pressure,
no goodbyes, no kiss of eye,
just fingers on the yellow pulse
of a digital computer,
codes for the car wash
yelled over the register.

Seize the day fill up let go.

IF I'M TO ANSWER

I do not speak of the new
in the uproarious chatter
of men who have forgotten
what they said last year.

Nicknames disowned—
one who boasted of his
can't remember its meaning,
coasts his eyes to lock it
in a new forgetfulness.

I'm always late,
always after the one
whose beginnings and ends
bundled neatly are tucked away.

I walk the ends of the porch
wearing a silly carnival hat,
it's a life time
of pacing the untouched,

dreaming of thin branches
that nod their heads
noiseless and delicate
as small, yellow butterflies.

Or I shuffle through
the slow rain of the afternoon
where autumn leaves play
mi casa, su casa,
birds in flight turn their necks
one last time to see me
as the evening sets to a murmur.

CAMPUS POET

Once again, ladies and gentlemen,
I've great pleasure in presenting myself—
The visiting poet is not visiting
Since his wife has threatened him
With curtailment of his visitation rights.
This time I'll read to you
The same poems you all know
By now by heart—
It's impossible to write new poems
Fast enough to read them each time
The visiting poet is not visiting.
However, I'll work on some new ones
After the series for the year comes to a close
Or we run out of money before it
Or we all grow damn sick & tired
Of visiting poets.
Let me begin today's reading
With the reading of my poem, Campus Poet.
I can see the very mention of it
Brings tears to your eyes
& you prepare yourselves to renew your stitches.
Thank you.
Afterwards I'll read
Just to keep your interest kindled
My sonnets without the numerals
So you'll have some fun guessing
Which one is which.
After the reading there'll be the usual party
At my place to which you & yours are invited.
However, I'd like to bring to your notice

It's high time we did something
About the parties I'm to throw
For the visiting poets not visiting.
Tonight there'll be draft beer
But please bring your own paper cup.
I'm sorry my wife will not be there
To receive you all graciously
Since she's babysitting
And you'll have to wait for me to let you in.
(Will someone drive me home?)
I'm afraid the party has to be short
As I'm substituting for the chairman
For the seminar on problems in modern poetry.
(Will someone give me a ride in the morning?)
I'd like to close this reading
With the reading of some translations
After which I'll be happy to accept your applause.
Also my thanks to the visiting poets
Whose not visiting has made my poetry prosperous
My tenure talked about.

STILL KICKING IN AMERICA

Now that I'm older,
the old ones ask
the same questions
the young ones asked
when I was younger.
You speak such good English?
How long have you been here?
An American Professor
dismisses my life story:
'Sounds just like my wife's,
she learned English
before coming here too.'
The wife dangling beside him,
jangles her earrings vehemently:
'Under communist regime,
all vodka going to dictators,
ration card, queue up,
legs getting very tired,
so I kicked the country,'
she says flipping her skirt
to let me peep at her
immense, strong-stemmed
proletarian calves.

Kicking a country
with such strong legs
is some kind of victory.
I look at my own shanks,

so thinned, so vegetarian,
even Gandhi would be shamed.
But these never kicked anyone
except their owner
in dreams or desperation,
hoping for words
to come out right in English.

SWANSONG

After the snowfall,
a blank sheet of paper
flutters in the alley between snow mounds.
A sudden draft must've blown it
from that open glass window,
the black neck of a swan
drooping on the windowsill.

G. S. SHARAT CHANDRA is a fiction writer and poet. His stories have received international attention. They have appeared in publications in England, the U.S. and India as well as in many anthologies, including *Winter's Tales* (London), *Writing Fiction* (Boston), and *Missouri Short Fiction*. Chandra is the author of five books of poems, most recently *Immigrants of Loss*. Currently a Professor of English at the University of Missouri-Kansas City, Chandra has also taught at Florida State University and Washington State. In 1989 he was Senior Fulbright Professor at Dhaka University in Bangladesh. He has been a visiting professor at Purdue and the University of Hawaii as well as Literary Editor of the *South Asian Language Review*. A graduate of the University of Mysore, India, and the University of Iowa, Chandra also holds law degrees from India and Osgoode Hall Law School in Toronto, Canada. He has given readings throughout the world: In England, Ireland, the U.S., Canada, Malaysia, Singapore, and India, including Oxford University and the Library of Congress.